FOURS & NINES
Quilted Placemats With Classic Blocks

By Wanda Hayes Eichler

Credits:
Photo styling and editorial assistance: Danielle Damen
Proofreading: Debbie Ballard, Danielle Damen, Jill Harmon, Patience McCarthy
Photography: Steve Jias, In Focus Photography
Illustrations and book design: Wanda Hayes Eichler

Special thanks:
Danielle Damen for her quilting skills and encouragement
MB Hayes for her innovative quilting notion, THANGLES
Patrick Mullen & Ed Eichler for their encouraging words

Published by Graywood Designs
P.O. Box 531
Pigeon, MI 48755
United States of America
www.quiltinpigeon.com
ISBN# 0-9779908-0-X

Copyright 2006. All rights reserved. No part of this book may be photocopied or reproduced without the written consent of Graywood Designs, Inc. All finished items produced from this book are protected by Federal Copyright Laws and may not be reproduced for commercial use in any form whatsoever without the express written consent of Graywood Designs, Inc. Published in the United States of America by Graywood Designs, Pigeon, Michigan.

INTRODUCTION

Have nothing in your house that you do not know to be useful, or believe to be beautiful.
William Morris

Ah, placemats! They're quick. They're easy. They're colorful. They entice us with their public nature. Placemats show up in our homes on the dining table. Placemats carry color and pattern and piecing and texture right into the heart of our homes – our kitchens and dining rooms.

Placemats slip onto a dresser top in a bedroom or out into the living room to top a side table. Placemats show up on the kitchen counter when a few wet dishes need a parking spot as they air dry. A placemat compliments a bouquet of flowers or a favorite candle. Like little quilts, they add that flavor of home to the most unexpected places.

Here is a collection of placemats designed with the look of traditional quilts. Starting with the building blocks of four-patch and nine-patch blocks and THANGLED half square triangles, these designs combine color and pattern to make placemats that you will enjoy using or giving as gifts.

Each pattern has a rating. One diamond for easy to make, two diamonds for designs that take a little more time, and three diamonds for projects that have the most piecing.

You will find directions, hints, and special techniques that I've developed for placemats. Most of these are detailed in the general directions. Included are a quick method of layering a placemat (or any other small project) and a specialized method of cutting bias strips for a placemat project.

None of the patterns are difficult, so wade in! Give your home a touch of quilting class as you choose colors and fabrics for new placemats. Enjoy!

Wanda Hayes Eichler
Pigeon, Michigan
Spring 2006

DEDICATION

This book is dedicated to my mother, Vallanee Rose Luedtke Hayes,
who taught me how to sew,

and to my mother-in-law, Pauline Beatrice Geiger Eichler,
whose quilts continue to inspire me.

Graywood Designs
Pigeon, Michigan   www.quiltinpigeon.com   888-453-4554

TABLE OF CONTENTS

General Directions

Two ruler method of cutting bias strips	4
Using THANGLES	5
Layering placemats	6
Binding placemats	6

Placemats with Four-patch blocks

Four Square & THANGLED ◆◆	8
Four By Four ◆	10
Prairie Queen ◆◆	12

Placemats with Nine-patch blocks

Six Nines & No More ◆◆◆	14
Sawtooth Nines ◆◆	16
Windmill Nines ◆◆	18

Quilting Suggestions

	20

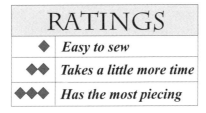

RATINGS	
◆	*Easy to sew*
◆◆	*Takes a little more time*
◆◆◆	*Has the most piecing*

GENERAL DIRECTIONS

Two ruler method of cutting bias strips

Stripes or checks or plaids cut on the bias bring interesting diagonal lines to bindings. Here's a quick method for cutting bias binding strips for placemats. Because you cut each strip separately, the stripes all run the same way. This method avoids the mirror image problems of cutting through layers and it places the diagonal seams away from the corners.

Use two rulers – 6" x 6" and 3" x 18." Using the same brand of ruler will give greater accuracy.

1. Start with a half yard of fabric (18" x 44"). Lay it out right side up in a single layer. You will be cutting from right to left, so begin on the far right side of the cutting mat.

2. Fold the upper right corner down to the bottom, forming a 45 degree diagonal fold.

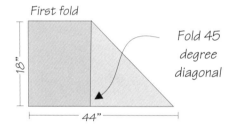

3. Fold the point of this diagonal up to the top of the fabric, doubling the fold.

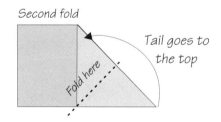

4. Place long ruler on left side of the fold. Make the first cut along the diagonal as shown through the four layers. Cut slowly and use your left hand to hold the ruler in place. When you can feel the rotary cutter slipping, put the cutter down and reposition your holding hand. Don't worry if this cut is a little "loppy" since bias is forgiving. A degree or two off of the 45 degree angle is okay.

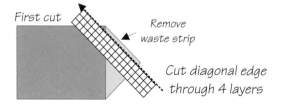

5. Unfold the fabric. Remove the large fabric triangle and set this aside. Refold the tail, matching cut edge to cut edge.

6. Place the small ruler so that the 2½" line is on the edge of the doubled fabric. Move it up and down to be sure that you have it aligned at the 2½" mark. Use your right hand to hold this ruler in place.

7. Using your left hand, pull the long ruler into place alongside the left edge of the small ruler. The long ruler now marks the cutting line that you have identified. You will cut along this ruler. Use your left hand as your holding hand. Pick up the rotary cutter and cut through both layers. The result should be the first bias cut strip.

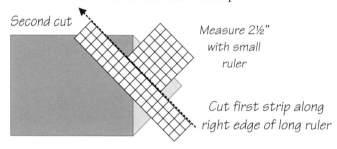

8. Repeat this process for the remaining strips. Realign the lower tail of the fabric as you cut strips from right to left.

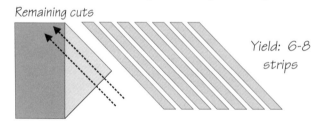

9. Depending on the width of the fabric, you will be able to cut 6-8 bias strips from a half yard cut. Cut 3 bias strips for each placemat you are making.

Using THANGLES

Half square triangles can be a challenge for many quilters. That's why there are so many techniques and products available that assist the sewing of an accurate half square triangle.

This book uses THANGLES. With this method you make half square triangle units from the same size of strips that you cut for squares and other pieces. Each THANGLE unit will give you two half square triangle units.

NOTE: If you are using the traditional cutting method for half square triangles, cut strips at 7/8" more than the size of the finished unit.

1. Place a light strip on top of a dark strip, right sides together. Pin the THANGLE template in place.

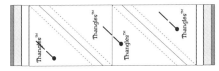

2. Stitch on the dotted lines.

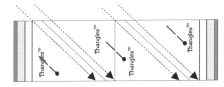

3. Cut on the solid lines.

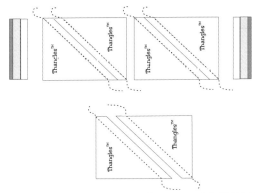

4. Press half square triangle unit open with THANGLE paper toward the pressing surface and trim one end.

5. Remove paper after pressing by holding paper in your left hand, creasing along the stitching, and tearing the paper.

More THANGLE Hints:

When you layer the strips with the light color on the top you will end up pressing the seam allowance toward the dark fabric.

Use a regular stitch length. THANGLES are made of a lightweight paper that will not dull a sewing machine needle. The paper tears away easily.

Press the half square triangle unit open before you tear the paper. The paper stabilizes the bias seam and prevents stretching.

Tear the paper by pinching the seam at the top of the unit and removing the paper.

One THANGLE paper makes 2 half square triangle units

Quilting Basics

Use 1/4" seam allowances.
Use rotary cutter, cutting mat, and see thru rulers.
Use 100% cotton quilting fabrics, 44-45" wide.
Use 100% cotton or 80% cotton/20% poly batting.

Layering placemats

Here's a rather casual method of layering placemats. Because placemats are small, this method does away with the usual basting and taping and securing. You can get away with less work when quilting placemats by using these hints.

1. **Use cotton batting.** Cotton adheres to cotton. It is like a magnetic attraction, so take advantage of this. Even the blended battings – 80% cotton/20% poly – have this characteristic.

2. **Use regular glass head pins to secure the layers together.** Avoid pins with long shanks and large heads. While they secure the layers well, it is easy to draw blood if you hit one while quilting. Use about 10-15 pins per placemat, no more. It takes time to put a pin into the layers and time to take it out. The fewer pins used, the more time saved.

3. **Work on a rotary cutting mat when pinning the placemat layers together.** Use an 18" x 24" mat. Dive the pin into the surface of the layers, drag the pin's tip on the mat surface and then make the pin reappear on top of the placemat.

4. **Be strict about the size of each layer.** The backing is the largest – it should always show so it can be controlled by tugging and pulling when stitching. The batting is slightly smaller. Keep ripples and folds under control by smoothing it often. If the batting is too large and you can't see the backing, trim the batting.

The piecing goes on top. Smooth all the layers with your hands and pin through the major seams. You can even pull the piecing to square it.

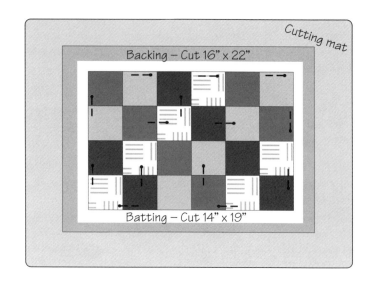

1. Working on a cutting mat, lay the backing down. Place the batting on top and then the placemat.

2. Pin through the three layers. Place pins around the edges and through major seams. Use as few pins as possible.

5. One last hint. Press the layers together lightly with an iron before you insert pins. The heat helps to seal the layers and works with the pins to keep them together. Work at an ironing board – don't press on a cutting mat.

Binding placemats

Binding adds the final touch to placemats. Whether you have chosen a subtle print cut crosswise or a bold plaid cut on the bias, the binding frames the piecing and finishes the work.

1. Trim the edges of the placemat through the quilted layers. Use a see thru ruler and rotary cutter. Trim 1/4" from line where binding will be stitched.

2. Join the 2½" binding strips by sewing diagonal seams right sides together. Trim seams to 1/4" and press open. For crosswise cut binding, you will sew two strips together; for bias cut binding, you will sew three strips together.

3. Press the binding in half wrong sides together lengthwise. Crosswise binding will be about 90" long. Bias cut binding will be about 75" long.

4. Fold the prepared binding in half and mark the center with a pin. If you are using crosswise binding, the pin marks the seam. If you are using a bias binding, the pin will be midway between the two seams.

5. Start pinning the binding to the right side of the mat by placing the center point of the binding to the center of the placemat. Align the raw edges of the binding with the raw edges of the placemat. Pin the corner miters and the edges. Miter the corners as shown.

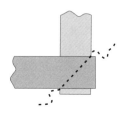

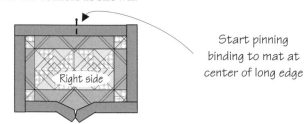

Start pinning binding to mat at center of long edge

Miter the corners

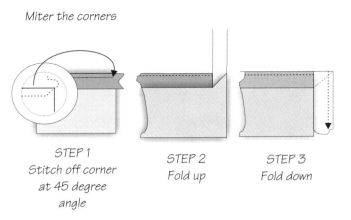

STEP 1
Stitch off corner at 45 degree angle

STEP 2
Fold up

STEP 3
Fold down

6. Start sewing 3" from a corner. Remove the pins as you come to the first corner so that you can stitch off the corner at the 45 degree angle. Take the placemat out from under the presser foot. Fold the binding to make the miter. Put the placemat back under the presser foot and backstitch ½" to secure the start of the stitching.

Continue stitching up to the second corner. Repeat the miter for each successive corner. Stop stitching 3" beyond the last corner.

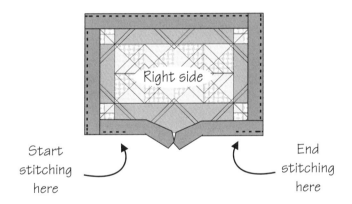

7. Place a marker pin at the center of the opening. Fold the loose ends of the binding up to this marker pin. The folded ends should be about 1/8" apart. Trim each end to 1 1/8".

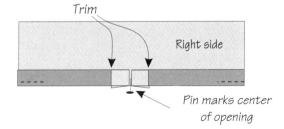

Fold each end of binding back at center point marked by pin. Trim ends.

8. Unfold the ends of the binding. You will be sewing a diagonal seam, right sides together. If the binding strips could be held freely, the seam would look like the drawing on the right. However, because the binding is already sewn in place, the binding ends will appear to be twisted.

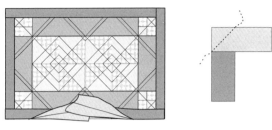

Unfold ends of binding

9. Pin this seam first to "audition" it. When you can see that you have pinned along the diagonal so that you are sewing a 45 degree seam and the seam allowance will be on the wrong side, sew the seam. Trim to 1/4." Press seam open.

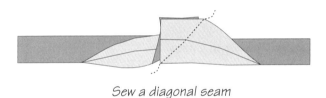

Sew a diagonal seam

10. Press last section of unstitched binding carefully, wrong sides together. Machine stitch binding to the placemat.

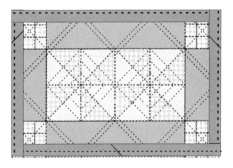

Finish sewing binding to placemat

11. For machine stitched binding, fold the binding to the back side, mitering the corners again. Pin on the back side. Press lightly. Pin in the ditch on the front side, removing pins from back. Stitch in the ditch slowly, removing pins as you come to them.

12. For hand stitched binding, fold the binding to the back side, mitering the corners. Pin. Using a milliners needle and regular weight thread, tack stitch the binding to back side of placemat.

FOUR SQUARE & THANGLED

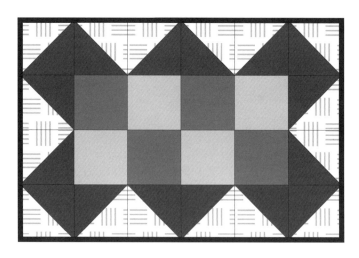

*Four-patch block size: 6" finished
Placemat size: 12" x 18"
Use 3.0" THANGLE*

Enjoy sewing four-patch blocks and lots of THANGLES in this easy design. You can change the look of the mat by reversing the position of the outside half square triangle units.

RATING: ◆◆

Fabric requirements for 4 placemats

Dark 1 – THANGLES:
  ½ yard
Dark 2 – four patch blocks:
  1/4 yard
Light 1 – THANGLES:
  ½ yard
Light 2 – four patch blocks:
  1/4 yard
Binding: Choose one
  Cut crosswise – 3/4 yard
  Cut on the bias – 1 yard
Backing:
  1 yard

Fabrics & Colors

Version One – Yellow & Green
*Dark 1 & 2: two green/yellow prints
Light 1 & 2: two green batiks
Binding: gold stripe, cut on the bias
Backing: medium green batik
Quilting thread: green, top & bottom*

Version Two – Blue
*Dark 1 & 2: dark blue marble, blue leaf
Light 1 & 2: blue rose print, blue streak
Binding: medium blue strips, cut bias
Backing: medium blue batik
Quilting thread: blue, top & bottom*

Cutting directions

For the outside half square triangles:
  From Dark 1, cut 4 – 3½" x 44" strips.
  Then cut 16 – 3½" x 11" strips.

  From Light 1, cut 4 – 3½" x 44" strips.
  Then cut 16 – 3½" x 11" strips.

For the four-patch blocks:
  From Dark 2, cut 2 – 3½" x 44" strips.
  Then cut 4 – 3½" x 22" strips.

  From Light 2, cut 2 – 3½" x 44" strips.
  Then cut 4 – 3½" x 22" strips.

For the backing:
  Cut 4 – 16" x 22" pieces.

*Bias binding**:*
  Cut 12 – 2½" x 25" bias strips as shown on page 4.
*Crosswise binding**:*
  Cut 8 – 2½" x 44" strips.

**Choose either bias or crosswise binding.

Layer, quilt, and bind according to the directions found on pages 5-7.

1 Piece the four-patch blocks

The four-patch blocks are strip pieced. You will need a total of 8 four-patch blocks, two for each placemat. Use half strips (about 22" long) that are easy to handle while sewing and pressing.

1. Using the 3½" x 22" strips that you have cut, make 3 strip sets by sewing the light and dark fabrics together. Sew right sides together. Press toward the dark fabric.

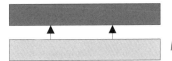

Sew a light strip to a dark strip
Make 3 strip sets

2. Using a rotary cutter and a see thru ruler, cut 3½" segments from each set. One 22" strip set makes 6 units. Cut 16 segments, two for each block.

Cut 6 – 3½" segments from each strip set
Cut 16 segments

3. Sew two segments together to make a four-patch block. Press seam one way. The block measures 6½" x 6½" unfinished. Make 8 four-patch blocks.

Blocks measure 6½" x 6½" unfinished

2 Piece the half square triangles

Use 3.0" THANGLES. If using another half square triangle method, be sure to cut strips as suggested for alternative method.

1. Using the 3½" x 11" strips that you have cut from the dark and light fabrics, make 64 half square triangles using 3.0" THANGLES. See page 5 for directions for using THANGLES.

Make 16 for each placemat
Make 64 for four mats

2. Each placemat uses 16 half square triangle units. Each unit measures 3½" x 3½" unfinished.

3 Assemble the placemats

1. Join two four-patch blocks together to make the center unit. This unit measures 6½" x 12½" unfinished.

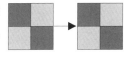

2. Sew four half square triangle units together to make top, bottom and side units. Press as shown.

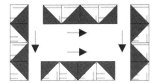

3. Sew the top and bottom units to the center. Press toward the center. Sew the sides to the center. Press toward the center. The unfinished placemat should measure 12½" x 18½" unfinished.

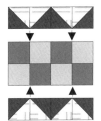 

Press in direction of arrows

4. Assemble the remaining three mats accordingly.

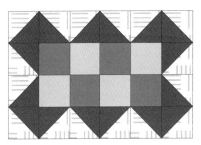

Layout as shown in directions

Alternate layout

Make this design look different by placing dark side of the THANGLE units along the edges of the mat.

FOUR BY FOUR

Four-patch block size: 6" finished
Placemat size: 12" x 18"

Four By Four is the easiest of all the designs in this book. Choose six fabrics – four for the piecing and two for binding and backing – and sew away!

RATING: ◆

Fabric requirements for 4 placemats

Dark 1 – four-patch blocks:
½ yard
Dark 2 – four-patch blocks:
½ yard
Light 1 – four-patch blocks:
½ yard
Light 2 – four-patch blocks:
½ yard
Binding: Choose one
Cut crosswise – 3/4 yard
Cut on the bias – 1 yard
Backing:
1 yard

Fabrics & Colors

Version One – Blue batiks
Dark 1 & 2: dark blue batiks with some pattern
Light 1 & 2: light blue batiks, almost no pattern
Binding: medium blue marble, cut crosswise
Backing: pale yellow print
Quilting thread: navy blue, top & bottom

Version Two – Red & Black Asian theme
Dark 1 & 2: gray print, black stripe
Light 1 & 2: two red batiks
Binding: red dot on black background
Backing: black butterfly on white
Quilting thread: black on top, red in bobbin

Cutting directions

For the four-patch blocks:
From Dark 1, cut 2 – 3½" x 44" strips.
Then cut 4 – 3½" x 22" strips.

From Dark 2, cut 2 – 3½" x 44" strips
Then cut 4 – 3½" x 22" strips.

From Light 1, cut 2 – 3½" x 44" strips.
Then cut 4 – 3½" x 22" strips.

From Light 2, cut 2 – 3½" x 44" strips
Then cut 4 – 3½" x 22" strips.

For the backing:
Cut 4 – 16" x 22" pieces.

*Bias binding**:*
Cut 12 – 2½" x 25" bias strips as shown on page 4.
*Crosswise binding**:*
Cut 8 – 2½" x 44" strips.

Layer, quilt, and bind according to the directions found on pages 5-7.

Six Nines & No More

Version 1

Pattern on pages 14 & 15

Elegant batiks mix with nine-patch blocks in this design that features a diagonal set.

Four Square & THANGLED
Version 1

Pattern on page 8 & 9

Green batiks and soft yellow prints accented with a gold stripe binding make this mat a delight.

Sawtooth Nines – Version 1 – Pattern on pages 16 & 17
This version of the Sawtooth Nines design showcases a large scale batik in a deep teal green.
Notice the use of the batik stripe cut on the bias for binding – a perfect finish!

Prairie Queen

Version 1

Pattern on pages 12 & 13

Here's the traditional prairie queen block with a mixture of one batik and several small scale prints.

*Antique dinnerware
from the collection of Karen Stacer Damen*

Windmill Nines – Version 2 – Pattern on pages 18 & 19
Bright prints set off the batik borders of Windmill Nines. The speckled, dotty print used for binding adds a funky touch to this version of the placemat.

Six Nines & No More

Version 2

Pattern on pages 14 & 15

Chili pepper fabrics combine with yellow and red nine-patch blocks to give this design lots of punch. Notice how the striped fabric cut on the bias adds lots of zing to the placemat.

RATING: ◆◆

Four Square & THANGLED
Pattern: pages 8 & 9
Photos: Cover, insert I
Yardage for placemat:
- Dark 1 – ½ yard
- Dark 2 – 1/4 yard
- Light 1 – ½ yard
- Light 2 – 1/4 yard

Use 3.0" THANGLES

RATING: ◆

Four By Four
Pattern: pages 10 & 11
Photos: Inside front cover, back cover
Yardage for placemat:
- Dark 1 – ½ yard
- Dark 2 – ½ yard
- Light 1 – ½ yard
- Light 2 – ½ yard

RATING: ◆◆

Prairie Queen
Pattern: pages 12 & 13
Photos: Insert II, inside back cover
Yardage for placemat:
- Dark 1 – ½ yard
- Dark 2 – 1/4 yard
- Light 1 – ½ yard
- Light 2 – ½ yard
- Medium – 1/4 yard

Use 4.0" THANGLES

RATING: ◆◆◆

Six Nines & No More
Pattern: pages 14 & 15
Photos: Insert I & III, back cover

Yardage for placemat:
- Dark 1 – 3/4 yard
- Dark 2 – ½ yard
- Light – ½ yard
- Medium – ½ yard

RATING: ◆◆

Sawtooth Nines
Pattern: pages 16 & 17
Photos: Insert II, inside cover
Yardage for placemat:
- Dark – ½ yard
- Light – ½ yard
- Medium 1 – 3/4 yard
- Medium 2 – 1/4 yard

Use 3.0" THANGLES

RATING: ◆◆

Windmill Nines
Pattern: pages 18 & 19
Photos: Inside cover, insert III
Yardage for placemat:
- Dark – ½ yard
- Light – ½ yard
- Medium – ½ yard

Use 3.0" THANGLES

1 Piece the four-patch blocks

The four-patch blocks are strip pieced. You will need a total of 24 four-patch blocks, six for each placemat. Twelve of the blocks use dark 1 and light 1; the remaining 12 blocks use dark 2 and light 2. Use half strips (about 22" long) for the blocks. Half strips are easy to handle while sewing and pressing.

1. Using the 3½" x 22" strips that you have cut, make strip sets by joining dark print 1 and light print 1. Press toward the dark fabric. Sew 4 strip sets.

2. Layer two strip sets right sides together with the light print on top.

3. Using a rotary cutter and a see thru ruler, cut 3½" segments from the layered sets. One 22" strip set makes 6 units.

4. Sew two segments together to make a four-patch block. Press these seams to the **left**. The block measures 6½" x 6½" unfinished.

5. Make 12 four-patch blocks of dark 1 and light 1.

Sew 12 blocks from dark 1 and light 1
Press center seam *left*

Sew 12 blocks from dark 2 and light 2
Press center seam *right*

6. Repeat these directions using dark 2 and light 2, again making 12 four-patch blocks. Press the seam in the second set of blocks to the **right**.

HINT: The dark fabric is in the upper left of each block. Keep track of the left corner of each block by placing a pin on the upper left dark fabric.

2 Assemble the placemats

1. Join three four-patch blocks together to make the top row. This unit measures 6½" x 18½" unfinished. Follow the diagram for block placement.

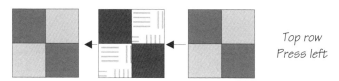

Top row
Press left

2. Sew three more blocks together for the bottom row.

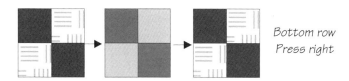

Bottom row
Press right

3. Finally, join the upper row to the lower row. The placemat should measure 12½" x 18½" unfinished.

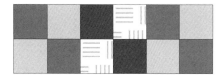

Center seam
Press up

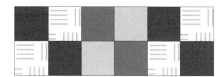

4. Assemble the remaining three mats accordingly.

PRAIRIE QUEEN

Four-patch block size: 4" finished
Placemat size: 12" x 18"
Use 4.0" THANGLE

Here's the Prairie Queen block centered in a placemat that has old fashioned charm and contemporary zing. Use batiks with small prints to create a mat with great eye appeal.

RATING: ◆◆

Fabric requirements for 4 placemats

Dark 1 – four-patch blocks & THANGLES:
  ½ yard
Dark 2 – four-patch blocks:
  1/4 yard
Light 1 – THANGLES & side panels:
  ½ yard
Light 2 – four-patch blocks, center & side panels:
  ½ yard
Medium – four-patch blocks:
  1/4 yard
Binding: Choose one
  Cut crosswise – 3/4 yard
  Cut on the bias – 1 yard
Backing:
  1 yard

Fabrics & colors

Version One – Peach, green, red, yellow
Dark 1 & 2: two green prints
Light 1 & 2: peach batik, yellow dot
Medium: rusty red print
Binding: rusty red print   Backing: yellow dot print
Quilting thread: gold on top, tan in bobbin

Version Two – Green, brown woodland
Dark 1 & 2: brown stripe, green batik
Light 1 & 2: tan acorn, black pinecone
Medium: beige print
(NOTE: black print in center is in LIGHT position)
Binding: subtle check, cut bias
Backing: green pine cone print
Quilting thread: green, top & bottom

Cutting directions

From Dark 1:
  Cut 1 – 2½" x 44" strip for four-patch blocks.
  Then cut 16 – 2½" x 2½" squares.
  Cut 1 – 4½" x 44" strip for THANGLES.
  Then cut 4 – 4½" x 11" strips.

From Dark 2:
  Cut 1 – 2½" x 44" strip for four-patch blocks.
  Then cut 16 – 2½" x 2½" squares.

From Light 1:
  Cut 2 – 4½" x 44" strips.
  Then cut 4 – 4½" x 11" strips for THANGLES.
  Also cut 8 – 4½" x 3½" pieces for side panels.

From Light 2:
  Cut 2 – 4½" x 44" strips.
  Then cut 4 – 4½" x 4½" squares for centers.
  Also cut 8 – 4½" x 3½" pieces for side panels.
  Cut 1 – 2½" x 44" strip for four-patch blocks.
  Then cut 16 – 2½" x 2½" squares.

From Medium:
  Cut 1 – 2½" x 44" strip for four-patch blocks.
  Then cut 16 – 2½" x 2½" squares.

For the backing:
  Cut 4 – 16" x 22" pieces.
*Bias binding**:*
  Cut 12 – 2½" x 25" bias strips as shown on page 4.
*Crosswise binding**:*
  Cut 8 – 2½" x 44" strips.
**Choose either bias or crosswise binding.*

1 Piece the four-patch blocks

1. Using the 2½" x 2½" squares that you have cut, sew a dark 1 square to a medium square. Sew a dark 2 square to a light 2 square. Press toward the dark fabric.

Sew dark 1 square to medium square
Press toward dark

Sew dark 2 square to light 2 square
Press toward dark

2. Now join the two segments to make a four-patch block that measures 4½" x 4½" unfinished. You can press this seam up or down. Make 16 four-patch blocks, four for each placemat.

Make 16 four-patch blocks
Blocks measure 4½" x 4½"

2 Piece the side panels

1. Using the 3½" x 4½" pieces that you have cut, sew the side panels using light 1 and light 2 as shown. Press toward the center.

2. The side panel measures 3½" x 12½" unfinished. Make 8 of these units, two for each placemat.

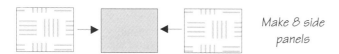
Make 8 side panels

3 Piece the half square triangles

Use 4.0" THANGLES. If using another half square triangle method, be sure to cut strips as suggested for alternative method.

1. Using the 4½" x 11" strips that you have cut from dark 1 and light 1, make 16 half square triangles using 4.0" THANGLES. See page 5 for directions for using THANGLES.

2. Each placemat uses 4 half square triangle units. Each unit measures 4½" x 4½" unfinished.

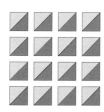
Make 16 half square triangles

4 Assemble the placemats

1. Join the half square triangles, four-patch blocks, and center square to make the center block. This unit measures 12½" x 12½" unfinished. Press according to the arrows.

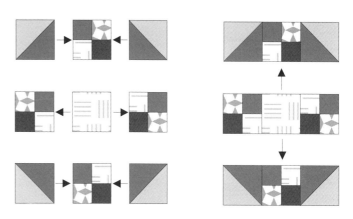

2. Sew the side panel units to the block. The placemat should measure 12½" x 18½" unfinished.

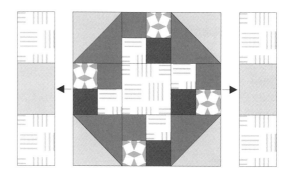

3. Assemble the remaining three mats accordingly.

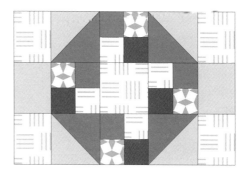

Layer, quilt, and bind according to the directions found on pages 5-7.

SIX NINES & NO MORE

RATING: ♦♦♦

Nine-patch block size: 3" finished
Placemat size: 12 3/4" x 17"

Six nine-patch blocks (and no more!) set the center stage for a diagonal design that is stunning. Don't let all the pieces seem daunting – it's really quite easy!

Fabric requirements for 4 placemats

Dark 1 – setting triangles, center squares:
  3/4 yard
Dark 2 – nine-patch blocks:
  1/2 yard
Light – setting squares:
  1/2 yard
Medium – nine- patch blocks:
  1/2 yard
Binding: Choose one
  Cut crosswise – 3/4 yard
  Cut on the bias – 1 yard
Backing:
  1 yard

Fabrics & colors

Version One – Purple, pale lime, teal
Dark 1 & 2: black batik, purple figured batik
Medium: teal figured batik
Light: pale lime batik
Binding: multicolor stripe with black, cut bias
Backing: purple & teal batik
Quilting thread: teal on top, lavendar in bobbin

Version Two – Red & black chili peppers
Dark 1 & 2: black chili pepper print, red print
Medium: yellow print
Light: red chili pepper print
Binding: red strip with yellow accent, cut crosswise
Backing: red chili pepper print
Quilting thread: red, top & bottom

Cutting directions

From Dark 1:
  Cut 2 – 5½" x 44" strips.
  Then cut 10 – 5½" x 5½" squares and then cut these squares twice diagonally for 40 setting triangles.

  Next, cut 2 – 3½" x 44" strips.
  From these strips, cut 8 – 3½" x 3½" center squares.

  Also cut 8 – 3½" x 3½" squares and then cut these squares once diagonally for 16 corner triangles.

From Dark 2:
  Cut 6 – 1½" x 44" strips for nine-patch blocks.
  Then cut 12 – 1½" x 22" strips.
From Light:
  Cut 4 – 3½" x 44" strips.
  Then cut 40 – 3½" x 3½" squares.
From Medium:
  Cut 6 – 1½" x 44" strips for nine-patch blocks.
  Then cut 12 – 1½" x 22" strips.
For the backing:
  Cut 4 – 16" x 22" pieces.
Bias binding**:
  Cut 12 – 2½" x 25" bias strips as shown on page 4.
Crosswise binding**:
  Cut 8 – 2½" x 44" strips.

**Choose either bias or crosswise binding.

1 Piece the nine-patch blocks

The 3" nine-patch blocks are strip pieced. You will need a total of 24 blocks. We will use half strips (about 22" long) because they are easy to handle when sewing and pressing.

1. Using the 1½" x 22" strips of dark 2 and medium fabric that you have cut, sew strips to make sets as shown. Press carefully in the direction of the arrows.

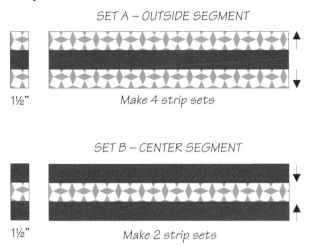

2. Layer one Set A (outside of block) & one Set B (center of block) right sides together. Using a rotary cutter and a see thru ruler, cut 1½" segments from the layered sets. Keep segments layered so you can sew the pieces together. One 22" strip set makes 13 layered units.

3. Cut 13 segments from the remaining Set A (outside of block) strip sets.

4. Sew the segments together. Press seams toward the outside of the block. Make 24 blocks. Each block measures 3½" x 3½" unfinished.

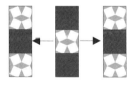

Each block measures 3½" x 3½" unfinished

Layer, quilt, and bind according to the directions found on pages 5-7.

2 Assemble the placemat

Sewing a diagonal design is easy when you subdivide the work into rows. Follow the diagram and the pressing suggestions for best results.

1. Sew each row together as shown. Press toward the plain squares.

2. Now sew the rows together. Press the seams all one way. The placemat measures about 13 1/4" x 17½" unfinished.

Press seams all one way when sewing rows together

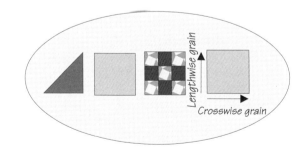

HINT: Align the lengthwise grain of each plain square as shown in the closeup. This takes advantage of the slight stretch of the crosswise grain when joining rows.

SAWTOOTH NINES

Nine-patch block size: 3" finished
Placemat size: 12" x 18"
Use 3.0" THANGLE

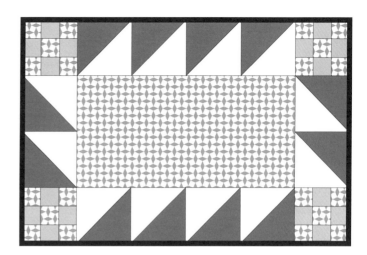

Four fabrics are featured with four nine-patch blocks in this design. Choose a stunning center fabric and the half square triangles will provide the traditional sawtooth accent.

RATING: ◆◆

Fabric requirements for 4 placemats

Dark – THANGLES:
 ½ yard
Light – THANGLES:
 ½ yard
Medium 1 – center, nine-patch blocks:
 3/4 yard
Medium 2 – nine-patch blocks:
 1/4 yard
Binding: Choose one
 Cut crosswise – 3/4 yard
 Cut on the bias – 1 yard
Backing:
 1 yard

Fabrics & colors

Version One – Teal & green
Dark: green check
Light: soft green
Medium 1 & 2: leaf batik, mottled green
Binding: teal batik, cut bias
Backing: mottled green print
Quilting thread: deep green on top, tan in bobbin

Version Two – Yellow, orange, green
Dark: orange print
Light: yellow floral
Medium 1 & 2: green/yellow/orange batik, orange batik
Binding: yellow/gold, cut bias
Backing: yellow dot on gold
Quilting thread: gold on top, tan in bobbin

Cutting directions

For THANGLES:
 From dark, cut 2 – 3½" x 44" strips.
 Then cut 8 – 3½" x 11" strips.

 From light, cut 2 – 3½" x 44" strips.
 Then cut 8 – 3½" x 11" strips.

For nine-patch blocks:
 From medium 1, cut 3 – 1½" x 44" strips.
 Then cut 6 – 1½" x 22" strips.

 From medium 2, cut 3 – 1½" x 44" strips.
 Then cut 6 – 1½" x 22" strips.

For center panels:
 From medium 1, cut 2 – 6½" x 44" strips.
 Then cut 4 – 6½" x 12½" pieces.

For backing:
 Cut 4 – 16" x 22" pieces.

Bias binding**:
 Cut 12 – 2½" x 25" bias strips as shown on page 4.
Crosswise binding**:
 Cut 8 – 2½" x 44" strips.

**Choose either bias or crosswise binding.

Layer, quilt, and bind according to the directions found on pages 5-7.

1 Piece the nine-patch blocks

The 3" nine-patch blocks are strip pieced. You will need a total of 16 blocks. We will use half strips (about 22" long) because they are easy to handle at the machine and when pressing.

1. Using the 1½" x 22" strips of medium 1 & 2 fabrics that you have cut, sew strip sets as shown. Press carefully in the direction of the arrows.

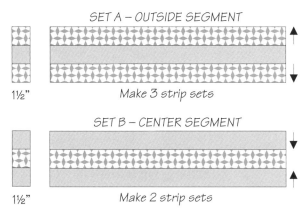

2. Layer a Set A (outside) & Set B (center) right sides together. Using a rotary cutter and a see thru ruler, cut 1½" segments from the layered sets. Keep segments layered so you can sew the pieces together. One 22" strip set makes 13 units.

3. Cut 13 segments from the remaining Set A (outside) strip sets.

4. Sew the segments together. Press seams toward the outside of the block.

Each block measures 3½" x 3½" unfinished

5. Make 16 blocks.

2 Piece the half square triangles

Use 3.0" THANGLES. If using another half square triangle method, be sure to cut strips as suggested for alternative method.

1. Using the 3½" x 11" strips that you have cut from the dark and light prints, make 48 half square triangles using 3.0" THANGLES. See page 5 for directions for using THANGLES.

2. Each placemat uses 12 half square triangle units. Each unit measures 3½" x 3½" unfinished.

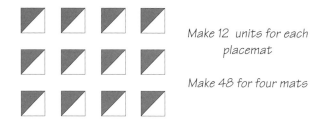

Make 12 units for each placemat

Make 48 for four mats

3 Assemble the placemats

1. Assemble the top, bottom, and side half square triangle units by sewing THANGLE units together. Press in the direction of the arrows.

2. Sew nine-patch blocks to each end of a top and bottom unit. Press as shown.

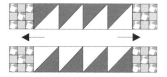

3. Sew the side half square triangle units to the center panel. Press toward the center.

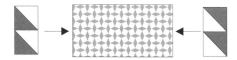

4. Join the rows and press as shown. The placemat should measure 12½" x 18½" unfinished.

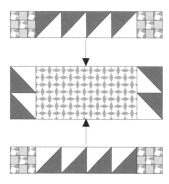

5. Assemble the remaining three mats accordingly.

WINDMILL NINES

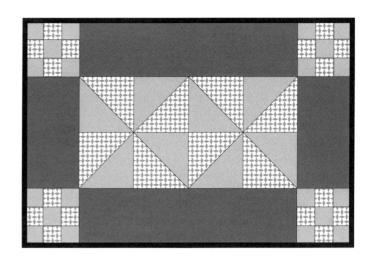

Nine-patch block size: 3" finished
Placemat size: 12" x 18"
Use 3.0" THANGLE

Two classic windmill blocks, three fabrics, and four nine-patch blocks make this an easy design to construct. The pieces are almost the same as Sawtooth Nines, but the effect is quite different!

RATING: ◆◆

Fabric requirements for 4 placemats

Dark – top & bottom, side borders:
  ½ yard
Light – nine-patch & windmill blocks:
  ½ yard
Medium – nine-patch & windmill blocks:
  ½ yard
Binding: Choose one
  Cut crosswise – 3/4 yard
  Cut on the bias – 1 yard
Backing:
  1 yard

Cutting directions

For THANGLES:
  From light, cut 2 – 3½" x 44" strips.
  Then cut 8 – 3½" x 11" strips.

  From medium, cut 2 – 3½" x 44" strips.
  Then cut 8 – 3½" x 11" strips.

For nine-patch blocks:
  From light, cut 3 – 1½" x 44" strips.
  Then cut 6 – 1½" x 22" strips.

  From medium, cut 3 – 1½" x 44" strips.
  Then cut 6 – 1½" x 22" strips.

For borders:
  From dark, cut 4 – 3½" x 44" strips.
  Then cut 8 – 3½" x 12½" pieces
  Also cut 8 – 3½" x 6½" pieces.

For backing:
  Cut 4 – 16" x 22" pieces.

Bias binding**:
  Cut 12 – 2½" x 25" bias strips as shown on page 4.
Crosswise binding**:
  Cut 8 – 2½" x 44" strips.

**Choose either bias or crosswise binding.

Fabrics & colors

Version One – Blue & gold
Dark: dark blue batik
Medium: blue/taupe batik
Light: gold marble
Binding: gold dot on black, cut crosswise
Backing: dark blue batik
Quilting thread: gold on top, navy in bobbin

Version Two – Teal, lime, fuschia
Dark: teal/green batik
Light: lime swirl
Medium: lime/fuschia/black floral
Binding: tiny lime dots on black
Backing: medium lime dots on black
Quilting thread: bright green, top & bottom

1. Piece the nine-patch blocks

The 3" nine-patch blocks are strip pieced. You will need a total of 16 blocks. We will use half strips (about 22" long) because they are much easier to handle at the machine and when pressing.

1. Using the 1½" x 22" strips of medium and light fabrics that you have cut, sew strip sets as shown. Press carefully in the direction of the arrows.

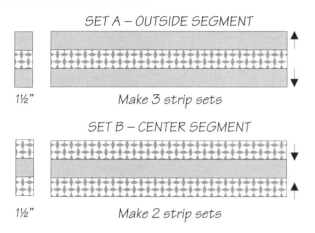

2. Layer a Set A (outside) & Set B (center) right sides together. Using a rotary cutter and a see thru ruler, cut 1½" segments from the layered sets. Keep the segments layered so you can sew the pieces together. One 22" strip set makes 13 units.

3. Cut 13 segments from the remaining Set A (outside) strip sets.

4. Sew the segments together. Press seams toward the outside of the block.

5. Make 16 blocks.

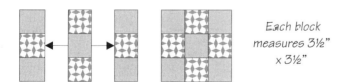

Each block measures 3½" x 3½"

2. Piece the half square triangles

Use 3.0" THANGLES. If using another half square triangle method, be sure to cut strips as suggested for alternative method.

1. Using the 3½" x 11" strips that you have cut from the light and medium prints, make 32 half square triangles using 3.0" THANGLES. See page 5 for directions for using THANGLES.

2. Each placemat uses 8 half square triangle units. Each unit measures 3½" x 3½" unfinished.

Make 8 units for each placemat

Make 32 for four mats

3. Assemble the placemats

1. Sew two nine-patch blocks onto the ends of the top and bottom border pieces. Press as shown.

2. Sew the half square triangles into the windmill blocks. Press as shown.

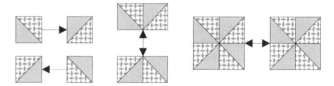

3. Join the two windmill blocks and the side border pieces.

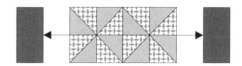

4. Join the rows and press as shown. The unfinished placemat should measure 12½" x 18½" unfinished.

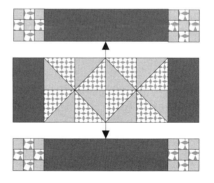

5. Assemble the remaining three mats accordingly.

Layer, quilt, and bind according to the directions found on pages 5-7.

QUILTING SUGGESTIONS

1. Use a chalk wheel pen. Mark lines only when needed. Brush the chalk away as soon as the line is quilted.

2. Use 12/80 machine needles that are sharp. Two possible choices are jeans or microtex needles. These needles pierce the layers efficiently and sew straight lines.

3. Use heavy thread in the needle and regular weight thread in the bobbin. By using two weights of thread, the tension is balanced in favor of the top thread. Most machines can handle this method.

4. Use a walking foot. The walking foot works like a second set of feed dogs that travel across the surface of the layers. Start quilting by pulling up the bobbin thread and taking 3 or 4 small stitches. Then set the stitch length to 8-10 stitches per inch (2.6 – 2.8 on computerized machines). Instead of backstitching, end with several small stitches.

5. Take a machine quilting class. Local quilt shops offer hands on instruction and advice that can make written directions come to life.

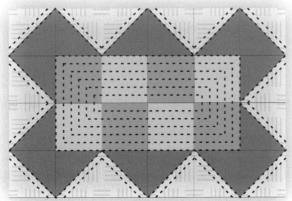
Four Square & THANGLED – pages 8-9

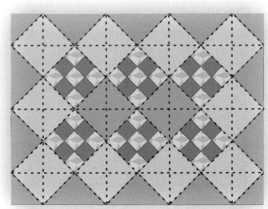
Six Nines & No More – pages 14-15

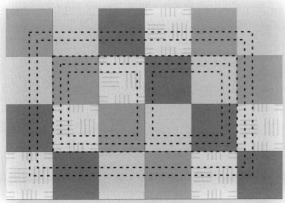
Four By Four – pages 10-11

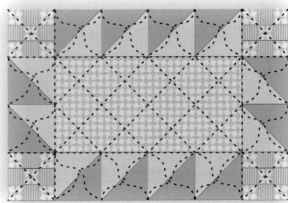
Sawtooth Nines – pages 16-17

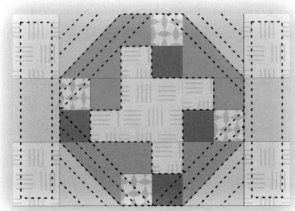
Prairie Queen – pages 12-13

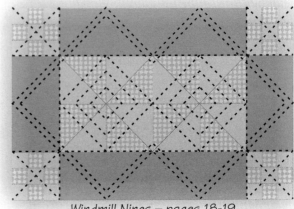
Windmill Nines – pages 18-19